11 habits of women who are never broke

Becoming financially unbreakable

Copyright © 2024 kelvin A. wealth

All rights reserved. No part of this publication may be reproduced, distributed, or transmitted in any form, including photocopying, recording, or other electronic or mechanical methods, without the publisher's prior written permission, except for brief quotations embodied in critical reviews and certain other noncommercial uses permitted by copyright.

INTRODUCTION

CHAPTER 1

Budgets have a poor reputation

CHAPTER 2

Needs vs. Wants
Diamonds are forever, but groceries aren't.

CHAPTER 3

The Goal Getter
Transforming Your Dreams into Financial Reality

CHAPTER 4

The Debt Destroyer
Breaking the Shackles and Seizing Financial Freedom

CHAPTER 5

The Income Maximizer
Increase Your Value and Slay the Salary Negotiation Dragon

CHAPTER 6

The Wise Woman Invests
Planting Seeds Today, Harvesting Abundance Tomorrow

CHAPTER 7

The Side Hustle Queen

Unleashing Your Inner Entrepreneur and Turning Passions into Paychecks

CHAPTER 8

The Insurance Illuminator
Protecting Your Dreams from Life's Unexpected Storms.

CHAPTER 9

The Automatic Annie—Set It and Forget It
Conquering Your Finances Using Automation

CHAPTER 10

The Empowering Network
Surround Yourself with Financial Fierceness

CHAPTER 11

The Abundant Mindset
You Deserve Financial Freedom.

CONCLUSION

Financially Fierce Forever

Introduction

Have you ever considered skipping the next budgeting meeting at work, where fluorescent lights hum above and spreadsheets taunt your shrinking savings? Perhaps you fantasize about silencing that nagging inner voice that asks, "Can you really afford that?" Imagine a world where financial anxiety does not keep you awake at night—a world where you make the decisions, not your bank account.

This, my friend, is the world of a financially strong woman. Forget the tired fairytales in which the prince appears on a white horse (or a symbolic high-paying job) to solve all your financial problems. Financial freedom is not about luck or hoping for a knight in shining armor. It's all about strategy, self-belief, and changing the story of your financial life.

Consider yourself the heroine of a riveting story, not a damsel in distress. This book will serve as your guide and compass as you navigate the thrilling, if often perilous, environment of personal finance. We will abandon the outdated clichés of sacrifice and hardship in favor of a path of empowerment and opportunity.

Here's the truth, financial freedom isn't some magical monster reserved for the wealthy few. It's a state of mind that enables you to take charge of your finances and make them work for you. Consider the possibilities of exploring the world without the continual stress of overspending, finally leaving that soul-crushing work, or pursuing your business goals without fear of financial ruin.

Financial freedom allows you to create a life on your terms, one full of experiences and stability.

However, the way to financial ferocity is not paved with magical fairy dust. It necessitates a dedication to studying, strategizing, and, most importantly, overcoming the limiting assumptions that have held you back. Perhaps you believe you are "not good with money" or that financial success is just for those born with a silver spoon. These are merely murmurs in the wind, my friend, which we will learn to mute together.

This book will teach you the 11 fundamental behaviors performed by women who have changed their financial stories. We'll look at budgeting that feels empowered rather than restricting, how to argue for the raise you deserve, and how to invest your money so it grows even while you sleep.

However, financial fierceness is more than simply statistics and techniques. It is about developing an abundance attitude and believing that you deserve and can reach financial security. We'll address the limiting thoughts and negative self-talk that keep us stuck and replace them with affirmations that will move you ahead in your financial journey.

So, are you prepared to change your financial story? Are you ready to ditch the damsel in distress and become the financially savvy heroine you were born to be? Let us turn the page and go on this empowering journey together!

CHAPTER 1

Budgets have a poor reputation

They bring up visions of dusty spreadsheets, endless rows of red numbers, and the crushing disappointment of being told "no" to everything you ever desired. But what if I told you that a budget may be your secret weapon, the key to achieving financial freedom and defeating the dreaded "money monster" that lurks in the shadows of your bank account?

Consider your budget to be a tailored guide to your financial goals, rather than a restricted cage. It's about becoming aware, understanding where your hard-earned money goes, and making intentional decisions that correspond with your goals and dreams.

Here's the thing: Most of us spend foolishly, propelled by impulse purchases and emotional responses. We swipe our cards or click "buy now" without thinking twice, only to be confronted with a sense of guilt (and a lighter pocketbook) later. Budgeting is the solution to financial forgetfulness. It's about shedding light on your spending habits, discovering opportunities for improvement, and, eventually, gaining control of your financial future.

But where should we even begin? Fear not, wannabe budget boss! We'll look at budgeting applications and cost trackers, which will serve as your trusted companions on this financial journey. These digital tools can be your hidden weapon, allowing you to categorize your spending, analyze your progress, and pinpoint areas where you can become a lean, mean, saving machine.

Let's speak about the benefits of categorizing your expenses. Think of your money as a scrumptious dessert. Each slice represents a separate category, such as rent or mortgage, groceries, utilities, or entertainment. Now, examine your spending habits to determine where the largest chunks are going. Are you indulging in too much "impulse buy" frosting? It's time to modify the recipe!

A good budget is flexible rather than inflexible. Life throws curveballs at you, and your budget should be flexible enough to handle them. Unexpected expense? Not a problem! Simply tweak another category (maybe that "designer shoe" splurge can wait another month) to keep your finances in order.

Remember, becoming a budget boss does not imply deprivation. It's about making deliberate decisions that move you closer to your goals. Do you fantasize about a nice trip to Italy? Allow your budget to reflect that desire by designating a set amount for a "travel fund." Perhaps financial independence means having the peace of mind to leave your stressful job. Begin creating a "dream fund" by allocating a portion of your salary.

This chapter focuses not just on the "how" of budgeting, but also on the "why." We'll look at the psychology of spending and identify the hidden emotional triggers that lead us astray. We'll learn how to recognize and avoid impulsive purchases, replacing them with deliberate judgments that correspond to your financial objectives.

By the end of this chapter, you'll have the information and tools you need to turn your budget from a chore into a valuable tool for financial empowerment. No more hiding from your bank statements; you'll be wielding them with the confidence of a financial ninja, ready to defeat the money monster and achieve your financial objectives!

Now let's get down to business! Here are some actionable strategies to help you start your Budget Boss journey:

The Great Expense Roundup: Gather your bank statements, credit card bills, and any other receipts that reflect your spending habits. This may seem frightening, but believe me when I say that addressing your financial reality is the first step toward positive change.

Categorize your conquest: Organize your spending into categories, such as accommodation, transportation, groceries, entertainment, and debt repayment. Many free budgeting programs have pre-made categories, or you can design your own to meet your requirements.

Track Every Move: For at least a month, keep meticulous records of your daily spending. This will provide you with a true view of where your money goes, from the morning espresso to the evening movie ticket. Budget boss, honesty is crucial!

"Needs vs. Wants" Showdown: Now it's time to face reality. Examine your group expenditures. Are there any places where you frequently surpass your budget? Are there "wants" masquerading as "needs"? Be ruthless. Identify places where you may cut costs to fund your financial goals.

Embrace the Power of "No": We've all heard the siren song of impulse buying. However, a firm "no" now can result in a booming "yes" to your future aspirations.

Create coping strategies for rejecting temptations. Perhaps a 24-hour cooling-off period before any non-essential purchase or a "treat yourself" fund set aside in your budget for intentional indulgence.

Remember, becoming a budget boss does not require perfection. It's about progress. There will be setbacks, times when the "money monster" attempts to rear its ugly head. However, with each mindful decision and monitored spending, you will acquire confidence and control over your finances. So, grab your metaphorical financial sword (aka budgeting app) and get ready to battle the monster! You, my friend, are on your way to becoming a financially formidable force to contend with!

Budget Hacks for Financial Fierce

Conquering the fundamentals of budgeting is an excellent starting point, but our journey to financial strength does not end there. **Let's look at some ninja-level tweaks that will improve your Budget Boss game:**

50/30/20 Rule: This budgeting technique divides your income into three categories: 50% for necessities (housing, groceries, and utilities), 30% for wants (entertainment, dining out, and hobbies), and 20% for savings and debt repayment. This framework is a wonderful place to start, but remember that you can alter the percentages to suit your specific needs.

Embrace automation: Technology is your friend! Set up automatic transfers into your savings and investment accounts. This "pay yourself first" strategy assures that you are continually building your financial fortress, even if you don't always realize it.

The Cash Envelope System: This may seem dated, but for some, it is a game changer. Set aside particular amounts of cash for different categories, such as grocery shopping or dining out. When the envelope is empty, spending in that category ceases—a tangible reminder to stick to your budget.

Renegotiate like a boss: Don't be hesitant to negotiate regular bills, such as cable or internet. Companies frequently provide discounts to loyal clients who are willing to bargain. This can free up a significant amount of money in your budget.

Embrace the power of "free.": There's an entire universe of free entertainment and activities waiting to be discovered. Visit local parks and museums during free entry days, or check your library's event calendar. Be creative and have fun without breaking the bank.

Remember that being a budget boss is an ongoing process. As your income increases or your financial goals change, review your budget and make any adjustments. Budgeting is your road map to financial independence, and a flexible plan is necessary for any epic adventure.

So, there you have it. You now have the knowledge and tools to face the money monster and unleash your inner financial ninja. Remember that financial ferocity is a journey, not a destination. Accept the obstacles, appreciate your accomplishments, and, most importantly, have fun along the way! The world of financial independence beckons, and you, my friend, are prepared to conquer it!

Chapter 2

Needs vs. Wants

Diamonds are forever, but groceries aren't.

Oh, the alluring tune of shopping therapy. That sense of immediate fulfillment as you swipe your card, the excitement of the new, and the promise of bliss tucked within that designer bag (or that third pair of shoes you "absolutely need"). But, let's be honest, ladies, these transitory pleasures frequently come at a high cost, one that might derail your ambitions of financial independence.

The ability to distinguish between requirements and wants is essential for financial ferocity. Needs are the non-negotiable, the necessities that keep your life operating smoothly: a roof over your head, nutritious food on your plate, and dependable transportation. Wants, on the other hand, are shiny objects whispering sweet nothings into your ear—the latest technology, the trendy dress, the impromptu weekend excursion (which your bank account may not be quite happy with).

The gremlins of financial stability, as I like to call them, are those deceptive wants masquerading as necessities. They play on our emotions, our need to keep up with the Joneses, or simply our enjoyment of a good shopping spree. Remember when you "needed" a pair of diamond earrings, even though your rent was due? Or the "essential" luxury handbag that made your grocery budget beg for air? We've all been there, my friend.

But here's the good news: becoming a financially strong woman necessitates mastering the art of saying "no" to these gremlins. It's about identifying your spending triggers and devising tactics to counteract them.

Perhaps you're a sucker for a good deal, believing that a 70% discount justifies purchasing something you don't need. Perhaps stress buying is your kryptonite; a hard day at work leads to a maxed-out credit card. Understanding your trigger is the first step towards overcoming it.

Here are some battle techniques to prepare you for your struggle against the Gremlins:

The 24-Hour Rule: Before giving in to the attraction of that "must-have" item, set a 24-hour cooling-off time. Give it some time to settle. When you revisit the purchase with a clear mind, the initial excitement usually fades and logic takes over.

The Needs List vs. the Wants List: Maintain a running inventory of both necessities and wants. When the impulse to splurge arises, refer to this list. Is this item a genuine requirement that contributes to your well-being, or only a passing fancy?

Answer to "Does it align?" Test: Each purchase should be considered in light of your financial objectives. Is this within your budget for an ideal vacation? Will it slow down your debt repayment? Making mindful decisions that match your long-term goals is critical.

Embrace the power of "enough.": Develop a sense of contentment. Appreciate what you already have and understand that true happiness does not come from material items. This shift in viewpoint will make it much easier to avoid impulse purchases.

Let's talk about the elephant in the room

FOMO (fear of missing out). Social media bombards us with photos of seemingly flawless lives, complete with the latest trends and expensive adventures. It's easy to feel envious and believe that "everyone else" has everything. But remember, dear reader, that social media is a highlight reel, not reality. Do not compare your behind-the-scenes experience to someone else's crafted feed.

Instead, surround yourself with like-minded people on their road to financial independence. Sharing your problems and enjoying each other's achievements creates a sense of community and holds you accountable. Remember that you are not alone in this war against the Gremlins.

Financial tenacity is not about denying oneself. It's about appreciating the finer things in life while remaining within reason. **Here are some ways to indulge mindfully:**

The Waiting Game: Prepare yourself to wait for sales and clearance events before purchasing a non-essential item. Patience is a great instrument that can drastically minimize the financial cost of your desires.

Consider valuing unforgettable experiences over material things. A weekend getaway with friends or a cooking class might help you make memorable memories while staying within your budget.

The DIY Divas: Get creative! Discover the world of DIY projects and crafts. A handcrafted costume or hand-decorated present can be more meaningful (and less expensive) than a store-bought option.

Mastering the skill of discernment will change you from a passive consumer to a mindful spender, allowing you to make decisions that are in line with your financial goals and genuine requirements. Remember that diamonds may last forever, but groceries (and financial security) are necessary for a meaningful existence. So, go on, Financially Fierce Woman! Conquer the gremlins, quiet the whispers of **FOMO**, and reinvent your financial story. Your future self, with a well-stocked pantry and a strong bank account, will appreciate it!

The weekly "Needs vs. Wants" Audit: Plan a weekly "needs vs. wants" audit. Examine your previous purchases and categorize them honestly. Did you prey on any sly gremlins? Analyze your triggers to find areas for improvement. Celebrate your accomplishments; every intentional decision is a step toward financial independence! Remember that progress, not perfection, is the aim.

So, there you have it. You now have the information and tools to become a discriminating, financially ferocious woman. By mastering the art of necessities vs. wants, you'll be able to enter a world of conscious spending and pave the road for a future full of financial security and freedom to pursue your ambitions. Let the journey begin!

Chapter 3

The Goal Getter

Transforming Your Dreams into Financial Reality

Ah, dreams. Those glittering dreams of a well-lived life and a future brimming with sunshine and possibility. Perhaps it's a picture-perfect vacation to a distant location, the pleasure of discovering old ruins or drinking drinks on a lovely beach. Perhaps your fantasy is of a tiny retirement cabin situated by a peaceful lake, with the calm rhythm of nature as your constant friend.

Whatever your heart wishes, my friend, financial freedom will open the door to those ambitions. However, if left unrestrained, dreams are like wisps of smoke. They require a structure—a blueprint—to translate their transient desires into actual realities.

This, my fellow financially strong woman, is where goal-setting comes into play.

Forget imprecise statements like "I want to travel more" or "I wish I could retire early." Let us transform these whispers into war yells! This chapter will provide you with the tools you need to set your financial goals with laser focus and create a clear and concrete plan to achieve them.

Introspection is the initial step on your path to achieving your goals. Grab a comfortable chair, and a steaming cup of your favorite beverage, and turn off the outside world. What ignites your soul? What experiences give me joy and a sense of fulfillment? Is it about discovering different cultures or spending quality time with loved ones? Identifying your basic beliefs is critical since your financial goals should eventually support the lifestyle you choose.

How does financial freedom look for me? Is it a freedom to pursue a passion project? The opportunity to travel the world without financial constraints? Defining your vision of financial freedom will act as a guiding light throughout your journey.

What are my financial priorities? Do you want to retire early or become a homeowner? Understanding your priorities will allow you to manage your resources more effectively.

Once you've started on this road of self-discovery, it's essential to turn your ambitions into tangible goals. This is where the SMART framework comes in.

Specific: Don't simply say, "Travel more." Instead, plan "a two-week trip to Italy within the next three years."

Measurable: How much will the trip cost? How much do you need to save each month to meet this goal? Establish explicit benchmarks to monitor your success.

Attainable: Be ambitious, but practical. Don't set yourself up for failure by attempting an unattainable goal. Break down enormous ambitions into smaller, more manageable milestones.

Relevant: Make sure your goals are consistent with your broader principles and vision of financial freedom.

Time-bound: Set explicit deadlines for completing each target. This generates a sense of urgency and keeps you motivated.

Now let's get down to business! Here are some actionable actions to help you transition from a dreamer to a goal-achieving machine:

The Vision Board Bonanza: Gather magazines, and newspapers, or search the internet for images that depict your ambitions, such as an Italian villa, the ideal retirement cabin, or a global map with destination circles. Creating a visual depiction of your goals helps you stay focused and motivated.

Power of "Why": Dig deeper than "I want this." Connect your goals to a greater cause. Do you want to explore the world, see new cultures, and broaden your horizons? Is early retirement about spending more quality time with your family? Understanding the "why" behind your goals will help you stay engaged during times of doubt.

The Reverse Budgeting Blitz: Let's imagine your ideal vacation to Italy costs $5,000. Set a deadline (remember, time-bound goals!) and calculate how much you can realistically save each month. This "reverse budgeting" strategy ensures that you allocate the finances required to make your aspirations a reality.

The accountability ally: find a friend or family member who understands your financial difficulties. Share your ambitions and hold one another accountable. Celebrate each other's accomplishments and offer support when faced with obstacles.

Remember that the path to reaching your financial goals will not always be smooth. There will be unforeseen expenses, moments of uncertainty, and the constant desire to deviate from your strategy. The goal-getter's hidden weapon, however, is resilience. Do not let setbacks derail you. Analyze what went wrong, revise your approach as needed, and get back up with renewed determination.

Financial freedom is more than just having enough money; it also means being able to live the life you want. By harnessing the power of goal setting, you may transform your aspirations from faraway fancies into a road map for a future full of possibilities.

The Gratitude Gauntlet: Gratitude is a powerful motivator that helps you stay focused on your goals. Here's a challenge: every night before going to bed, take a moment to think about three things you're thankful for that day. It may be anything—a beautiful meal, a supportive companion, or simply the good fortune of being alive. By cultivating a grateful mindset, you will become more appreciative of what you currently have, making achieving your goals much more important.

So there you have it, my fellow financially strong woman! You now have the knowledge and tools to transform yourself into an expert goal-getter. Remember that dreams aren't luxuries; they're the fuel that drives you ahead. Accept the power of goal-setting, embrace the strength of resilience, and witness your ambitions transform from whispers to financial realities. The world awaits, full of adventures and encounters; go forth and conquer them all!

Chapter 4

The Debt Destroyer

Breaking the Shackles and Seizing Financial Freedom

Ah, debt. The four-letter word that sends shivers down even the most financially strong woman's spine. Student loans, credit card bills, auto payments—these obligations might feel like chains, holding you hostage and impeding your path to financial freedom.

But have no fear, dear friend! This chapter will provide you with the knowledge and methods you need to transition from a debt-ridden damsel to a debt-destroying dynamo. We'll look at powerful debt-reduction measures, smart negotiation skills, and, finally, how you can break free from debt and breathe the delicious air of financial freedom.

First and foremost, let us confront the beast directly. Gather all of your financial statements, including credit card bills and loan documentation. Disperse them across the table; this represents your formidable debt force, which you are prepared to vanquish. List each debt, including its outstanding balance, interest rate, and minimum payment. Knowledge is power, and understanding your debt environment is critical to developing an effective combat strategy.

Now let's talk about strategy! Here are two prominent techniques for overcoming debt:

The Snowball Method: prioritizes repaying the lowest obligations first, regardless of interest rate. The thrill of watching your bills go one by one can be a great motivator and keep you going on your debt-reduction quest. Once a debt is paid off, you may use the additional money to tackle the next biggest one, producing a snowball effect that builds momentum as you go.

The Avalanche Method: This technique prioritizes addressing loans with the highest interest rates first. While it may take longer to pay off smaller obligations, prioritizing high-interest debts will save you money in the long term.

The most appropriate strategy for you is determined by your personality and financial position. The Snowball Method can be a terrific motivator for individuals who want a rapid win; however, the Avalanche Method may be a superior long-term plan for those who prefer a delayed sense of fulfillment.

Here are some extra battle techniques to help you on your debt-reduction journey:

The Negotiation Ninja: Do not be scared to contact your creditors and negotiate! Explain your financial situation and ask if they'd be willing to cut your interest rate or minimum payment. The worst they can say is no, and the best-case scenario will save you a lot of money.

The Budget Bootcamp Revisit: Remember the fantastic budget you created in Chapter 1? Here's where it shines! Reassess your spending and discover places where you may cut back. Every extra dollar saved might be used to further your debt-reduction objective.

The Side Hustle Samurai: Consider starting a side venture to supplement your income and pay off debt. This could range from freelance employment to selling unused stuff online. Every penny matters in this war!

However, overcoming debt is more than simply numbers and techniques; it is also about a mental adjustment. Here are some mental armor plates to prepare you:

The "Goodbye FOMO" mantra: Debt destroys your future financial independence. Resist the tendency to buy on impulse and follow bright trends. Remember that true happiness does not come from worldly stuff.

The Importance of Delayed Enjoyment: Learning to prioritize long-term financial goals over immediate enjoyment is essential. The fleeting pleasure of a new purchase pales in contrast to the independence that comes with being debt-free.

The celebratory crusader: Recognize and appreciate your accomplishments, no matter how tiny! Have you paid off your credit card? Treat yourself to the non-budget experience you've been yearning for (within reason!). Rewarding yourself helps you stay motivated and reinforces good financial habits.

The journey to become a debt destroyer will not be simple. There will be temptations, disappointments, and days when the pile of debt seems insurmountable. Remember, you are not fighting this battle alone. There's a whole army of financially savvy ladies cheering you on!

Here are some other resources to help you along your journey:

The National Foundation for Credit Counseling provides free materials and advice on debt management.

Debt.com offers educational resources and methods for dealing with debt.

Find online or in-person support groups to meet people on the debt-free journey.

By using the tactics and adopting the mentality of a debt destroyer, you may change yourself from a debt prisoner to a financially empowered fighter. Consider the sensation of liberation—the ability to pursue your aspirations without the burden of debt holding you down. That's the strength you have within you, my friend. Now, go forth and achieve financial freedom!

The Debt-Destroyer Declaration

Here's a wonderful tool to strengthen your resolve to become a debt destroyer: Create a personalized Debt Destroyer Declaration. This is your battle cry and manifesto against debt. Write it down, place it somewhere you'll see it every day, and use it as a continual reminder of your goals.

Here's an example to help you get started:

I, [Your Name], declare war against debt! I will no longer be a slave to credit card debt and loan obligations. I plan to use budgeting, negotiating, and cautious spending as weapons. I will pay off my debt, one deliberate step at a time. Financial independence awaits, and I shall pursue it with zeal!

Remember that financial freedom is a journey, not a destination. There may be challenges along the way, but with steadfast determination and the tools you now have, you can become a debt destroyer and reclaim control of your financial destiny. So, take your figurative war paint (or perhaps a sassy highlighter) and prepare to rewrite your financial story! The world of financial independence awaits you; go forth and grasp it!

Chapter 5

The Income Maximizer

Increase Your Value and Slay the Salary Negotiation Dragon

Have you ever had that sinking feeling when you learn you're being paid less than your male coworkers for the same work? Perhaps you've worked extra hours and exceeded expectations, yet your raise barely covers the increased cost of food. Fear not, Financially Fierce Woman! This chapter is your rallying cry and guide to changing yourself from an underpaid underling to an income maximizer.

Let's be honest: income is the cornerstone of financial freedom. The more you earn, the more you may save, invest, and ultimately meet your financial objectives. However, simply working hard is not enough. You must be a strong advocate for your worth, a fearless negotiator who demands fair recompense for the value you bring to the table.

Here's the fact, honey: most firms do not give out increases like candy. They expect you to battle for them, demonstrate your value, and firmly explain why you deserve a larger share of the pie. So, let us prepare to unleash your inner income maximizer!

Know your worth, Queen.

The first step is becoming self-aware. Research compensation ranges for your employment, taking into account aspects such as experience, geography, and industry. Use online tools such as Glassdoor, or professional association websites to determine the market value of your talents and experience. This knowledge is your armor—your shield against lowball offers.

Become a Master in Your Craft

Never stop studying and developing your talents. Take online classes, attend industry conferences, and actively seek out possibilities for professional growth. The more valuable you are to your employer, the more powerful your negotiating position will be.

Document your achievements

Keep track of your accomplishments, such as projects finished ahead of schedule, excellent client comments, or exceeding sales targets. Concrete evidence of your contributions supports your desire for a raise. Don't be frightened to brag (figuratively speaking).

The Art of Confident Asking

Preparation is crucial. Schedule a meeting with your manager and come prepared with your research, your achievement record, and a clear notion of the raise you want. Prepare your pitch by rehearsing your points, anticipating any objections, and, most crucially, projecting confidence.

Focus on value, not just time.

Do not just state, "I've been here for X years, so I deserve a raise." Frame your request in terms of the value you provide to the organization. Highlight your effect, the challenges you've solved, and the revenue you've created. Make them understand that giving you a raise means investing in their future success.

Be prepared to walk away.

Know your bottom line. If the offer does not reflect your value, be prepared to walk away from the negotiation (figuratively speaking). Having additional options, even if only for leverage, enhances your position.

Remember that negotiation is a two-way conversation, not a war. Be professional, respectful, and receptive to counteroffers. Maybe a raise isn't the only choice.

Discuss extra advantages such as stock options, flexible work schedules, and enhanced paid time off.

Saying "no" to an undervalued offer can be powerful. Thank your management for their time, emphasize your worth to the firm, and recommend resuming the talk at a later date.

The Village behind Victory

Don't be afraid to seek guidance and help from mentors, coworkers, or even a professional negotiation coach. There's power in numbers, and having trusted counsel by your side can enhance your confidence and effectiveness.

Negotiations beyond the Raise

Salary negotiations are about more than just raises. It applies to all aspects of your working life. Negotiate your starting salary, benefits, and even your workload. By advocating for yourself, you demonstrate that you value your worth and will not accept anything less.

Becoming an income maximizer requires a mindset that goes beyond methods. It is about developing a mindset of abundance and self-worth. Believe in yourself, understand your abilities, and never be hesitant to ask for what you deserve.

Remember that financially strong women do not wait for opportunities; they create them. By adopting the tactics and mindset of an income maximizer, you may transition from an underpaid employee to a financially powerful force. You'll command respect, recognition, and recompense that match your genuine worth. Consider the sense of entering into a negotiation with unwavering confidence, knowing your worth, and demanding what you deserve. That's the strength you have within you, my friend.

The Negotiation Role play

Take a friend or colleague and role-play a salary negotiation scenario. Take turns acting as the employee and the manager, and practice your arguments and counterarguments. This practice session will enhance your confidence and prepare you for probable problems in a real-life negotiation.

By adopting the tactics and mindset of an income maximizer, you will defeat the salary negotiation dragon and uncover a future of financial security and the freedom to pursue your aspirations. Remember that knowledge equals power, and confidence is your weapon. Now go forth, Financially Fierce Woman, and prove your worth!

Chapter 6

The Wise Woman Invests

Planting Seeds Today, Harvesting Abundance Tomorrow

Ah, investment. The very mention of it may conjure up visions of Wall Street wizards spewing esoteric language into phones or sequences from fast-paced films where fortunes are made (and lost) in the blink of an eye. Fear not, Financially Fierce Woman! Investing does not have to be an intimidating, elite club. In reality, it's a powerful instrument that can help you grow your money enormously over time, bringing you closer to your goal of financial independence.

Consider it akin to planting seeds. You invest some of your hard-earned money today, cultivate it with patience and intelligent decisions, and over time, those seeds grow into a bountiful harvest that ensures your financial future. This chapter will provide you with the knowledge and confidence you need to transition from an inexperienced investor to a wise woman investor.

Let us remove the idea that investing is just for the wealthy. The truth is that everyone can get started, regardless of their budget. Even little amounts invested regularly over time can have a tremendous impact due to the magic of compound interest, which earns interest on both the initial principal amount and the cumulative interest over time. It's like gaining interest on your interest—a financial snowball that continues to rise the longer you let it roll.

Now, let's discuss investment choices. The financial world may seem like a foreign language, but don't be intimidated. Here's an overview of some common investment vehicles:

Stocks: Owning a portion of a corporation. When the company performs well, the stock price often rises, allowing you to potentially sell your shares for a profit.

However, stocks can be volatile, which means their prices might move dramatically.

Bonds: Essentially, you are lending money to a firm or government in exchange for a fixed interest rate over a specified time period. Bonds are often regarded as less risky than stocks, although they have fewer potential rewards.

Mutual funds are investment baskets that include stocks, bonds, and other assets. Investing in a mutual fund diversifies your holdings, which reduces risk.

Exchange-traded funds (ETFs) are similar to mutual funds, except they move throughout the day like stocks. They provide a low-cost option to obtain exposure to a wide range of assets.

Real estate can be a profitable investment, offering rental income as well as the opportunity for long-term capital appreciation. However, real estate necessitates a large initial investment and ongoing maintenance obligations.

Feeling overwhelmed? Do not worry! Here are some tools for the savvy woman investor:

Robo-advisors: These internet platforms offer automated investment management services for a lesser cost than traditional financial advisors. They ask you a series of questions about your risk tolerance and financial objectives before creating and managing a diverse portfolio for you.

Low-cost index funds: These passively managed funds follow a certain market index, such as the S&P 500. They provide an inexpensive solution to acquire broad market exposure without the requirement for individual stock selection.

Financial Literacy Resources: There are several online sites, books, and even workshops where you may learn the fundamentals of investing. The more you educate yourself, the more assured you will be when navigating the investment world.

Here are some important principles to know as a wise woman investor:

Start early: Compound interest has the greatest effect over time. The sooner you start investing, the longer your money has to grow.

Diversify, Diversify, Diversify: Avoid putting all of your eggs in one basket. Diversify your investments across asset groups to reduce risk.

Invest for the long haul. The stock market can be volatile, with ups and downs in the near term. Do not panic and sell your investments during a slump. Concentrate on the long-term growth potential.

Invest within your risk parameters Tolerance: Are you a risk-taker willing to accept future market volatility or a more conservative investor who values stability?

Understanding your risk tolerance will help guide your investment decisions.

Do Not Time the Market: Attempting to foresee market movements is a recipe for disaster. Maintain a consistent, long-term investment approach.

Seek professional advice (if needed): If you're feeling overwhelmed or unclear about your investment options, speak with a skilled financial counselor.

Becoming a wise woman investor is not about creating a get-rich-quick plan. It is about making sensible, informed decisions that will allow you to develop your money over time and achieve financial freedom. Remember, information is power. By educating yourself and taking action, you can change yourself from an investment innocent to a financially smart investor, watching your money grow and pave the way for a secure and abundant future.

The Investment Tracking Toolbox

There are various free and inexpensive investment tracking programs available online. These tools enable you to track your portfolio's performance, remain current on market developments, and rebalance your holdings as appropriate. Having a clear view of your investments allows you to make informed decisions and stay on track with your financial objectives.

By adopting the principles of a wise woman investor, you will sow the seeds of financial security now and receive the plentiful harvest of a successful tomorrow. Remember that financial freedom is not a privilege; it is a potential waiting to be realized. So, Financially Fierce Woman, grab your metaphorical gardening gloves and prepare to see your money flourish!

Chapter 7

The Side Hustle Queen

Unleashing Your Inner Entrepreneur and Turning Passions into Paychecks

Ladies, let's be honest, the 9-to-5 grind doesn't always cut it. Perhaps you want the freedom of being your own boss, the flexibility to work your own hours, or just more money to help you get closer to financial independence. That's where the power of the side hustle comes in!

Consider monetizing your interests and passions. Becoming a Side Hustle Queen is about more than simply generating money; it's about expressing your creativity, creating something you're proud of, and redefining the traditional job model on your own terms. This chapter will provide you with the knowledge and inspiration you need to unleash your inner entrepreneur and explore the enormous world of side hustles waiting to be discovered.

First and foremost, let go of your limiting beliefs! You do not need a fancy business degree or a lot of money to get started. To turn your interests into money, all you need is a dash of creativity, a sprinkle of hustle, and a strong determination.

Uncovering Your Side Hustle Goldmine

The initial step is self-discovery. What are you good at? What are you enthusiastic about? Do you have a talent for creating gorgeous jewelry? Perhaps you're an expert at creating show-stopping cakes? Perhaps you have a flair for other languages or enjoy penning engaging stories. These, my friend, are the beginnings of your potential side hustle empire.

Here are some side hustle ideas that will get your creative juices flowing.

The Freelancer: Offer your expertise in writing, editing, graphic design, virtual support, and social media management. Freelancers can connect with clients all over the world through websites like Upwork and Fiverr.

The Creative Maven: Make money from your artistic talents. Sell your handcrafted products on Etsy, create one-of-a-kind t-shirts on Redbubble, or provide bespoke calligraphy services.

The Knowledge Guru: Do you have a unique set of skills or expertise? You can share your knowledge by developing online courses, ebooks, or webinars. You can reach a global audience through platforms such as Udemy and Skillshare.

The Gig Economy Guru: Platforms such as TaskRabbit and Rover link people looking for odd jobs, pet sitting, or dog walking. It's a flexible method to earn money on your own time.

The Rent Revolution: Do you have a spare room in your house? Rent it out on Airbnb. Do you own a car that you don't use every day? List it on Turo. There are several options for monetizing unused assets.

From Idea to Income Stream

The Side Hustle Action Plan

After identifying a prospective side hustle, take steps to make it a reality. Here is your action plan:

Market research: examine the competitive landscape. Who are your potential clients? How much are they willing to pay? Understanding your market will allow you to refine your offering and set competitive prices.

Branding Basics: Even if you're just starting out, develop a professional brand identity. This might include a memorable name, a logo, and perhaps a basic website or social media presence.

Pricing Power: Research industry standards to determine your value proposition. Do not undervalue your abilities or knowledge. Remember that you are providing a valuable service or product.

Market Magic: Don't be scared to shout your side hustle from the rooftops (metaphorically speaking). Use social media channels, network with possible clients, and look into online advertising options to spread the word about your excellent offers.

The Legal Lowdown: Depending on your chosen side hustle, there may be legal or tax consequences. Do your study and make sure you're following the law.

The Side Hustle Mindset

Identifying a fantastic idea isn't enough to become a side hustle queen. It's about cultivating the appropriate mindset.

Embrace the hustle: Creating a successful side hustle requires dedication and consistent effort. Be prepared to work extra hours at first, but remember that the benefits outweigh the effort.

Learn and adapt: The business world is continuously changing. Be willing to learn new skills, tailor your offers to market demands, and always look for opportunities to improve.

Celebrate Milestones: Don't wait till you reach a six-figure income to celebrate your accomplishments. Recognize even the smallest achievements, such as landing your first client, finishing your first job, or exceeding your early income targets.

Find Your Tribe: Connect with other side hustlers! Online groups and forums provide important support, encouragement, and a platform for sharing ideas and experiences.

The Power of Side Hustle

The Side Hustle Queen's beauty lies in its adaptability. It's a tool for financial empowerment, a Launchpad for entrepreneurial ideas, and a path to a life tailored to your needs. It enables you to discover hidden abilities, create a brand around your passions, and add an extra dose of excitement and joy to your life.

Imagine the possibilities of using your side hustle money to pay down debt faster, save for a dream vacation, or achieve financial freedom. The power is within you, Financially Fierce Woman! Embrace the hustle, release your inner entrepreneur, and see your side hustle grow from a seed of an idea to a flourishing tree of financial freedom.

The Side Hustle Queen's Toolkit

There are numerous internet resources and tools to help you along your side hustle journey. Here are some suggestions to get you started:

Free online courses: Platforms such as Coursera and Skillshare provide free courses on marketing, branding, and social media management.

Project Management Applications: Tools like Trello and Asana may help you stay organized, manage projects efficiently, and keep your side hustle operating smoothly.

Accounting Software: Use user-friendly accounting software such as Xero or Quickbooks to track your income and expenses, making tax season a snap.

By arming yourself with the knowledge, tools, and unyielding attitude of a Side Hustle Queen, you can turn your hobbies into riches and unlock a future full of financial freedom and limitless opportunities. Remember, the only limitation is your imagination, Financially Fierce Woman! So, what are you waiting for? Go ahead and achieve your side hustle goals!

Chapter 8

The Insurance Illuminator

Protecting Your Dreams from Life's Unexpected Storms.

Life, my friend, is a lovely yet unpredictable adventure. One minute you're basking on the sun-drenched shores of your financial ambitions, and the next, a figurative storm cloud sweeps in, threatening to ruin your painstakingly planned strategies. Perhaps it's an unexpected medical cost, a sudden handicap that keeps you from working, or the unfathomable death of a loved one. These unexpected setbacks can make you feel vulnerable and financially exposed.

Fear not, Financially Fierce Woman! Just as a bold knight puts on armor to protect themselves in combat, you can empower yourself with a powerful shield—the shield of insurance. This chapter will elevate you from Insurance Innocent to Insurance Illuminator, allowing you to confidently traverse the world of insurance and select the best plans to protect your financial well-being and the dreams you hold dear.

Let's be honest, insurance may be a complicated maze of jargon and fine language. But here's the secret: understanding the fundamentals of insurance allows you to make informed judgments and select the best coverage for your individual needs.

Here is a breakdown of several major types of insurance

Health Insurance: This is your primary protection against the rising tsunami of medical bills. It protects you from the financial consequences of unforeseen illnesses, injuries, or hospitalizations. Different types of health insurance plans provide varying amounts of coverage, so choose one that is appropriate for your health needs and budget.

Life insurance: This may sound morbid, but it is not about concentrating on the negative. It is about providing financial stability for your loved ones if something terrible occurs. A life insurance policy provides a death benefit to your specified beneficiaries, allowing them to cover expenses and maintain financial security in your absence.

Disability Insurance: Life delivers curveballs, and these curveballs can take the form of an accident or illness that prohibits you from working. Disability insurance provides a source of income if you are unable to work due to a covered disability, allowing you to retain your financial stability during a difficult period.

Insurance Illuminator's Action Plan

Now that you have some basic knowledge about the various types of insurance, it's time to take action.

Needs Assessment: Before digging into policy, take a deep breath and examine your specific requirements. Consider your age, health, dependents, financial objectives, and lifestyle. This will assist you in selecting the appropriate type and level of coverage.

Shop around: Don't settle for the first offer you get. Compare quotes from various insurance companies to discover the best balance of coverage and price. Remember, the lowest policy is not always the best choice.

Decode the jargon: Do not be hesitant to ask questions! Insurance policies contain numerous technical terms and exclusions. Before you sign on the dotted line, make sure you understand the coverage details, restrictions, and potential out-of-pocket payments.

Review regularly: Your living conditions are continuously changing. As your needs change, make sure your insurance coverage is still appropriate for your present scenario.

The Power of Being Prepared

Having the correct insurance coverage may not prevent life surprises, but it can greatly reduce their impact. Consider the peace of mind that comes from knowing you've made efforts to financially secure yourself and your loved ones in the event of an unanticipated scenario. Insurance is more than simply numbers on a page; it is about protecting your dreams and providing financial security even when the unexpected occurs.

But here's the deal Financially Fierce Women. Your financial armory includes more than just insurance. By incorporating the strategies and mindsets discussed in this book—goal-setting, debt reduction, income maximization, wise investing, and the side hustle spirit—you'll create a strong financial fortress capable of enduring life's storms and propelling you toward a future brimming with security and freedom.

The Insurance Illuminator's Toolkit

There are various resources available to assist you as you navigate the world of insurance. Here are some suggestions to get you started:

Government Websites: The National Association of Insurance Commissioners (https://content.naic.org/) and the United States Department of Labor (https://www.dol.gov/) provide helpful information and consumer guides for many types of insurance.

Independent Insurance Agents: These professionals can assist you in determining your needs, comparing rates from numerous firms, and selecting the best insurance products for your specific scenario.

Online Comparison Tools: Websites such as [placeholder: insurance comparison website] enable you to compare rates from multiple insurance companies in one place, saving you time and effort.

By utilizing the knowledge of an insurance illuminator and carefully implementing the appropriate insurance products into your financial plan, you will transition from feeling vulnerable to feeling empowered. You'll confront life's uncertainties with unwavering confidence, knowing that you've created a financial safety net that preserves your aspirations and helps you to weather any storm that may arise. Remember, Financially Fierce Woman, that readiness equals power. So go forward, enlighten your road with insurance knowledge, and conquer your journey to a future full of security and peace of mind.

Chapter 9

The Automatic Annie—Set It and Forget It

Conquering Your Finances Using Automation

Ah, the human condition. We strive for efficiency, for systems that simplify and save us time. However, when it comes to our finances, many of us slip into a cycle of manual labor. We diligently track costs in notebooks, remember deadlines with crossed fingers, and move funds between accounts with a sigh of "there has to be a better way."

Fear not, Financially Fierce Woman! There is a better way, a wonderful path built with automation—your secret weapon in the fight for financial independence. This chapter will take you from Frazzled Financial Fighter to The Automatic Annie, a master of putting your finances on autopilot.

Consider this, you wake up every morning feeling empowered, knowing your financial well-being is being looked after without continual monitoring or mental stress. Automatic Annie automates the monotonous tasks of money management, allowing you to focus on your goals and objectives.

Power of Automation

Automation is equivalent to having a relentless financial assistant working for you around the clock. It removes the possibility of forgetting bills, missing investing opportunities, or falling behind on your savings goals. Automating repetitive chores allows you to:

Free up mental bandwidth: Stop spending your valuable brainpower remembering due dates and transfer amounts. Let automation handle the minutiae, allowing you to concentrate on larger financial goals and your overall financial well-being.

Increase consistency: Life gets busier. Automation guarantees that your financial obligations are met consistently, even when your schedule becomes hectic.

No more rushing at the last minute to transfer funds or pay debts.

Reduce the risk of human error: Let's be honest, we're all humans and prone to making mistakes. Automation reduces the danger of forgetting a payment or entering the incorrect amount.

Develop discipline: Setting up recurring transfers for savings and investments encourages a pattern of continuous financial growth. You'll see your wealth steadily increase without having to worry about it.

Automatic Annie's Toolkit

Now that you're convinced of the power of automation, let's look at the tools available to you:

Sign up for automatic bill payment through your bank or directly with your service provider. This ensures that your invoices are paid on time each month, avoiding late fees and any damage to your credit.

Automatic Savings Transfer: Schedule automatic transfers from checking to your savings account. This "pay yourself first" strategy ensures that a percentage of your income is constantly allocated to your savings goals, even before you have the opportunity to spend it.

Automated Investment Contributions: Many investment platforms include the option of setting up automatic investment contributions. This enables you to invest a set amount of money at regular intervals, much like clockwork. This method, known as dollar-cost averaging, allows you to profit from compound interest over time while also reducing the danger of investing a significant sum at the incorrect period of the market cycle.

Budget Apps with Automation Features: Several budgeting apps help you automate certain financial responsibilities. These capabilities can include automatic transaction categorization, setting spending restrictions, and even sending alerts when you're about to go over your budget.

Become an Automatic Annie

Here's your action plan to become a financial automation champion.

Identify your automation opportunities: Look for repetitive financial tasks that can be automated. This could involve bill payments, savings transfers, or even regular investment contributions.

Explore Your Options: Examine the automated options provided by your bank, investing platform, or budgeting tool. Many institutions provide simple interfaces for setting up automatic transfers and regular payments.

Embrace the "set it and forget it" mentality: After you've automated your financial responsibilities, take a deep breath and rest! Knowing that your finances are being handled automatically will provide you with peace of mind while also freeing up critical time and resources. However, it is important to recognize that automation is not a panacea. It is critical to check your automated transactions regularly and make any necessary adjustments based on your changing financial goals.

Financial Freedom Formula

Automation, when combined with the tactics covered in this book—goal setting, debt reduction, income maximization, sensible investment, and the side hustle attitude—allows you to develop a potent financial independence formula. Setting your finances on autopilot will help you achieve your financial goals without the stress and burden of manual management.

Consider the possibilities, Financially Fierce Woman: waking up every day with the assurance that your financial future is safe, knowing that your money is working for you while you sleep. Automation is the key to achieving financial freedom and peace of mind. So, go forth, harness the power of automation, and change into The Automatic Annie! Remember that financial freedom is not a pipe dream; it is a well-constructed strategy propelled by automation and empowered action. Take control of your money, put it on autopilot, and see your wealth grow as you navigate your way to a future filled with security and the flexibility to pursue your wildest goals.

The Automatic Annie's Resource Vault

There are several resources available to help you become an automation expert. Here are some suggestions to get you started:

Online Banking Tutorials: Most banks provide lessons and recommendations on how to use their online banking capabilities, such as automatic bill payments and savings transfers.

Investment Platform FAQs: Many investment platforms have thorough FAQs and help sections for setting up automatic investment contributions.

Budget App Reviews: Websites and financial blogs frequently provide budgeting app evaluations that highlight its automation features and user-friendliness.

You will transform your financial management by arming yourself with the knowledge and skills required to become an automatic Annie. Embrace the power of automation, Financially Fierce Woman, and watch your path to financial freedom speed!

Chapter 10

The Empowering Network

Surround Yourself with Financial Fierceness

Consider this Financially Fierce Woman: You're climbing the mountain of financial freedom, but the ascent appears difficult. Self-doubt comes in, and the summit appears far away. Suddenly, you hear a chorus of applause from behind. You turn to see a gathering of strong, supporting ladies cheering you on. This, my friend, is the strength of the Empowering Network.

Financial success is not an individual goal. It's a journey best undertaken with a supporting tribe by your side. This chapter will help you create a network of financially strong women who will inspire, encourage, and empower you on your journey to financial freedom.

Consider this, associating oneself with others who have similar financial goals produces a powerful synergy. You'll learn from each other's experiences, celebrate both major and small accomplishments, and hold each other accountable during difficult times.

The pillars of the Empowering Network

The ideal financial network is constructed around three main pillars:

Mentorship: Seek out a financial mentor, someone who has already accomplished the financial goals you desire. They may provide essential advice, share their hard-earned knowledge, and serve as a sounding board for your ideas and issues. Financial mentors can be located in professional groups, internet networks, and even within your social circle.

Accountability partners: Find a financially strong woman with a similar financial journey and build an accountability alliance. Regularly communicate your financial objectives and progress, hold each other accountable for sticking to your budgets, and applaud each other's accomplishments. This sense of shared accountability can be a powerful motivator, helping you stay on track to achieve your goals.

Supportive Community: Join a community of financially smart women. Online forums, social media groups, and local financial empowerment courses are all great venues to meet like-minded people. These groups provide an opportunity to share experiences, ask questions, and learn from others' financial adventures.

Building Your Empowering Network

Now that you understand the significance of a supportive network, here's how to create your own.

Leverage Online Resources: The internet is a gold mine for financial communities. Join Facebook groups dedicated to financial empowerment, follow inspirational women on social media, or engage in online forums focused on financial success.

Seek out mentoring programs: Many professional organizations and financial institutions have mentoring programs that connect aspiring individuals with experienced mentors. Conduct research and investigate potential options that correspond with your financial objectives.

Attend Financial Workshops: Local workshops or seminars on financial literacy are fantastic venues to interact with other women on the same journey.

Do not be afraid to ask: Do you have a financially knowledgeable buddy or coworker you admire? Approach them and communicate your desire to learn from their experiences. You might be astonished by their desire to mentor you or introduce you to their own network.

Strength of Shared Success

The beauty of the Empowering Network stems from the strength of shared experiences. By surrounding yourself with financially powerful women, you will gain:

Motivation: Seeing the success of others in your network will keep you motivated and inspired to pursue your own goals.

Knowledge Sharing: A supportive network allows you to learn from others' experiences and strategies, which accelerates your financial growth.

Accountability: Knowing that someone is rooting for you and holding you accountable will help you stay on track with your financial goals.

A Sense of Belonging: Financial empowerment can feel isolating. The Empowering Network offers a safe area to connect with people who share your goals and struggles.

The Final Climb to Financial Freedom

Creating a strong and helpful network is an investment in your financial success. With a community of financially strong women by your side, achieving financial freedom becomes less daunting and far more fulfilling. You'll celebrate successes together, overcome obstacles as a group, and eventually reach the pinnacle of financial freedom, fueled by the collective strength of your network.

Remember, Financially Fierce Woman, you're not alone on this road. Accept the power of The Empowering Network, connect with like-minded women, and watch as your financial goals become a reality, propelled by the combined strength and steadfast support of your financial tribe.

Consider this, you've reached the pinnacle of financial independence with your empowering network. The view is breathtaking—a vista of security and possibility reaching out in front of you. But keep in mind that reaching the summit is only the beginning of a new adventure.

This supporting network you've created becomes a lifelong resource. As your financial objectives change, so will the help you require from your network. Perhaps you'll shift your focus from seeking advice to mentoring those just starting. Perhaps you'll engage with your network to invest in enterprises together, leveraging your combined financial strength.

The possibilities are limitless, and the voyage continues. Financial freedom is more than just having a particular amount in your bank account; it is about living a life with purpose, security, and the opportunity to pursue your wildest goals.

So go forth, Financially Fierce Woman, and expand your empowering network. Accept the value of mentorship, accountability, and shared success. Remember, you are not alone. You and your tribe of financially savvy women can climb any financial mountain and take your rightful position at the pinnacle of financial freedom.

Develop a Financially Fierce Mindset

Beyond expanding your network, cultivating a financially strong mindset is critical for long-term success. Here are some strategies for cultivating a strong financial attitude:

Embrace Lifelong Learning: The banking industry is always growing. Commit to constant learning and remaining current on new trends and methods.

Celebrate Each Milestone: Don't wait until you've met your ultimate financial goal to celebrate. Recognize and praise yourself for each step forward, no matter how tiny.

Develop gratitude: Financial freedom allows you to live life on your terms. Practice thankfulness for your accomplishments and the changes that lie ahead.

Embrace setbacks as learning experiences. Everyone has financial challenges along the way. Setbacks can be used as learning opportunities to improve your strategy and increase your financial stability.

By using these principles and the empowering tactics presented in this book, you will transform from an investment innocent to a financially ferocious woman, ready to achieve your financial goals and live a life full of freedom and security. So take a deep breath, accept the trip, and realize that the path to financial freedom begins right now.

Chapter 11

The Abundant Mindset

You Deserve Financial Freedom.

Ah, Financially Fierce Woman, we've been through a significant amount of your financial journey. You've armed yourself with the tools and techniques needed to defeat debt dragons, overcome budgeting animals, and invest with the confidence of a seasoned warrior. But before you continue your journey to the pinnacle of financial freedom, there is one critical thing we haven't covered: your inner landscape.

This chapter digs into the heart of the matter: your thinking. Financial independence is more than simply numbers in a spreadsheet; it's about developing an "abundance mentality." It is about feeling deep down in your heart that you deserve financial security and have the ability to accomplish it.

Consider this: Your thinking is the rich soil in which the seeds of your financial objectives are planted. A scarcity mindset, filled with limiting beliefs and negative self-talk, generates a barren landscape in which seeds struggle to germinate. But build an abundance mindset, and your financial aspirations will thrive in a lush and fertile atmosphere.

From Scarcity to Abundance: Removing Limiting Beliefs

We all have baggage, my friend. Limiting beliefs—the whispers of doubt that tell you "you're not good enough" or "you don't deserve financial success"—can prevent you from reaching your full financial potential. Let us identify some common culprits:

"Money is the root of all evil." This restrictive mentality demonizes riches, making it impossible to achieve financial objectives. Remember that money is a tool that, like any other, can be utilized for good or harm. Financial freedom enables you to provide for your loved ones, pursue your passions, and make a meaningful contribution to society.

"I'm not good with money." This is a self-fulfilling prophecy. Instead, accept the notion that financial literacy is a talent that you can learn. This book is your guide, and there are other tools available to assist you on your journey.

"The rich get richer, and the poor get poorer." This scarcity mindset implies there is a finite supply of wealth. Financial freedom is attainable for everyone who is prepared to commit and study. Focus on your journey and enjoy the successes of others as they pave the way for your accomplishments.

Planting the Seeds of Abundance: Creating Empowering Affirmations

Now that we've pulled out the weeds of limiting thoughts, let's sow the seeds of an abundant mindset.

Here are some empowering affirmations to help you get started:

"I am worthy of financial abundance." Repeat this mantra regularly to remind yourself that you deserve financial security and the freedom that comes with it.

"I am financially capable." Recognize your natural skill to manage your cash efficiently. You've taken control of your financial journey, which is a significant first step.

"I am a magnet for abundance." Shift your emphasis from scarcity to prosperity. Visualize yourself attracting financial opportunities and accomplishing your goals.

"I am grateful for the financial abundance in my life, and more is on its way." Gratitude develops a happy perspective and opens the door to additional blessings.

Beyond Affirmations

Developing the Abundant Mindset

Affirmations are wonderful tools, but actual abundance takes ongoing nurture. Here are a few ways to build an affluent mindset:

Surround yourself with positive influences: Look for financially knowledgeable people who exemplify this abundant concept. Their success stories and great attitude will motivate you throughout your trip.

Practice visualization: Take time each day to see yourself accomplishing your financial objectives. Imagine yourself living a life of freedom and security. The power of imagination can train your subconscious mind to succeed.

Celebrate your wins, big and small: Recognize your progress, no matter how tiny it may appear. Celebrating your accomplishments encourages healthy behaviors and keeps you encouraged throughout your path.

Concentrate on what you can control: Don't squander energy on issues beyond your control, such as the stock market or the economy. Concentrate on the things you can control, such as your spending habits, money-generation techniques, and investment decisions.

The key to long-term success is having an abundant mindset

The abundant mindset is more than just financial independence; it is about living a life full of wealth in all its manifestations. It's about having the means to pursue your passions, give back to your community, and explore the globe on your terms. It's about developing a sense of gratitude for everything you have and the confidence to live the life you desire.

By implementing the tactics discussed in this chapter and throughout the book, you may transition from a financially fragile woman to a financial warrior with an abundant mindset. Remember that abundance is a journey, not a destination. There will be moments of uncertainty and setbacks, but with a strong sense of self-worth and a supporting network by your side, you will weather any storm. Accept the trials, learn from your failures, and never lose sight of the prosperous life that awaits you at the pinnacle of financial freedom.

The ripple effect of abundance

Financial freedom is not a solo goal; it has the potential to ripple outward, resulting in positive change. Creating abundance in your own life inspires people around you. Perhaps you'll help others navigate their financial adventures, or you'll utilize your newfound security to support great organizations. The options are limitless. Remember that financial freedom allows you to not only live the life you want but also to contribute to a more prosperous society for everyone.

Your abundant future awaits

This book has provided you with the knowledge, tools, and techniques necessary to overcome your financial anxieties and attain the freedom you deserve. But remember, Financially Fierce Woman that the road never truly ends. Financial freedom is a lifelong quest, a constant journey of learning, growing, and adjusting. Accept the continual process, appreciate your triumphs, and never lose faith in your capacity to create a prosperous future.

Go forth, Financially Fierce Woman, and take your rightful place at the pinnacle. The world awaits the magic you'll make with the power of financial independence.

Conclusion

Financially Fierce Forever

Congratulations, financially strong women! You've concluded this empowering trip. But keep in mind that this isn't your typical happily-ever-after fairy tale. It's the starting point for a lifelong metamorphosis, a blazing inferno of financial ferocity that will light your road to a future brimming with stability and freedom.

Financial freedom isn't a fixed location on a single mountain peak. It's a huge and bright landscape that changes with each season of your life. There will be moments when you can't believe how far you've come. However, there will undoubtedly be valleys of uncertainty, with unanticipated financial storms building on the horizon.

The rollercoaster of financial freedom

The habits and mindset you've developed throughout this book will help you navigate this ever-changing landscape. Remember, setbacks are unavoidable. An unexpected medical expenditure could disrupt your budget for a month. The stock market may fall, creating a temporary decline in your investments. These are not signals of failure; rather, they are minor setbacks.

The Financially Fierce Women's Toolkit

The tools you've gathered throughout your journey will enable you to weather any financial storm:

Your Budget Blueprint: Your precisely created budget serves as a financial road map, guiding you through unexpected detours and keeping you on track for your long-term objectives.

The Debt Slayer Strategy: The knowledge you've received allows you to approach debt with renewed vigor, chipping away at those annoying responsibilities and freeing up vital resources for the future.

The Investment Arsenal: You've discovered the secrets of smart investing, which allows you to use compound interest and expand your wealth over time, even during market changes.

The Automatic Annie's efficiency: Automation simplifies your financial life, freeing up mental space and guaranteeing that your financial obligations are paid continuously, even when life is chaotic.

Empowering Network's Strength: Your tribe of financially strong women provides continuous support, guidance, motivation, and a safe space to celebrate successes and overcome obstacles.

The Abundant Mindset's Power: You've developed a belief system that allows you to manifest financial wealth in your life. This foundation of self-belief and thankfulness drives your determination and pulls you onward in times of doubt.

Embrace the journey, not just the destination.

Remember, there is beauty in the journey itself. As you negotiate the financial landscape, you'll learn essential life lessons, build resilience, and gain renewed confidence in your abilities to handle your money. Celebrate little achievements like sticking to a weekly budget, paying off a credit card, or attaining a savings goal. These moments of progress lay the door for even greater success.

The Financially Fierce Legacy emphasizes that financial independence extends beyond the individual. It is about establishing a legacy of financial literacy and empowerment. Share your expertise with your loved ones, guide others through their financial adventures, and encourage a new generation to rewrite their financial narrative. Breaking the cycle of financial illiteracy helps to create a future in which financial security is a birthright rather than a privilege.

This book is coming to an end, but your financial journey is far from over. Go forth, Financially Fierce Woman, with a restored sense of purpose and a heart filled with financial ferocity. Embrace the journey, rewrite your ending, and take your rightful place in a world of financial independence and endless opportunities. Remember that you have the power to build a life you enjoy. You are in control of your financial fate. Write your tale with confidence, resilience, and unshakable financial tenacity. The world eagerly awaits the magic you'll create.

www.ingramcontent.com/pod-product-compliance
Lightning Source LLC
Chambersburg PA
CBHW050317230526
45471CB00005B/2231